An Anthology

Of Fables

**An Anthology
Of Fables**

ISBN 978-1-908419-91-0

A CIP record is available at the British Library

Made in 1961 by NJP Wegner (NP James from 2002)
Facsimile scanned from the original in 2013

This is a digital format publication
Printed and bound by Blissett: Design.Print.Media
www.blissettdigital.co.uk

Cv Publications
www.tracksdirectory.co.uk

Introduction

As a child he would sometimes go upstairs to the studio where his father, a renowned children's book illustrator, worked. He would stand beside him watching pencil roughs evolve into finished studies of intimate detail; the little figures and settings hatched with a scratching dip pen, some tinted with colour washes. He was occasionally used as a model for reference of children, drawn or painted in outfits, once posed as a young shepherd in a red cloak with a staff.

From seven years old he would bring his drawings and watercolours for inspection; then at twelve years he made his first book: an anthology of fables and poems copied from shelves of literature, embellished with pen drawings.

Saved by his sister over the years this resurfaced. To mark his father's 89th birthday a facsimile is published, in fond tribute and gratitude for those special beginnings.

NPJ September 2013

Contents

An anthology

WAGNER

THE FROG AND THE OX

A great ox, grazing in a swamp, put down his foot on a family of young frogs, and crushed most of them to death. One escaped, and ran off to tell his mother the terrible news. Mother, he said, you never saw such a big beast as the beast that did it! Big? said the foolish old mother frog. She puffed herself to twice her size, and said, Was it as big as this? Oh no, Mother, much, much bigger. She puffed herself some more, and said, As big as this? Oh no, Mother, much much bigger. So she puffed again, and puffed so very hard that suddenly with a great POP!! she burst into little pieces.

SMALL MEN CAN DESTROY THEMSELVES BY STRIVING TO BE BIGGER THAN THEY ARE

THE ROOSTER & THE EAGLE

Two young roosters were fighting fiercely over a worm. Finally one of the Roosters was badly beaten and was covered in wounds, so he ran away and hid in the henhouse. The conqueror, proud of his victory, flew to the top of the henhouse to tell the world about it. But an Eagle had been wheeling around above the henhouse, waiting for a chance to catch himself some dinner; and no sooner did the Rooster start to crow, than the waiting Eagle swooped down, and carried him away.

DON'T CROW IN FAST COMPANY.

THE TORTOISE & THE EAGLE

A tortoise was not satisfied with living in a little pond, when he saw his friends the birds flying where they pleased. He thought that he could learn to fly too, and asked the Eagle to take him up so he could learn. The Eagle told him he was mad; But the tortoise begged and bothered him, and assured him he could fly. Finally the Eagle agreed, and carried the tortoise high into the air. Are you high enough now? cried the Eagle, looking back at his vain friend, the Tortoise. But the tortoise, although frightened to death, opened his mouth to boast that he wanted to go higher, and thus lost his hold, and fell down, down, to his death.

PRIDE COMETH BEFORE THE FALL

THE HORSE AND THE GROOM

A groom used to steal a horse's corn and yet was very busy in grooming and currying him all day long. Said the horse:

IF YOU REALLY WISH ME TO LOOK WELL, WORRY LESS ABOUT MY SKIN, AND MORE ABOUT MY STOMACH.

THE SICK COW

An old cow was afraid he was dying, so he said to his children: Go out and pray that I may recover. Ah, Father, said the young cows To which god shall we pray? for you have spent your lifetime robbing the altars of them all, and taught us to do the same

A DEATHBED REPENTANCE IS POOR,
AMENDS FOR A BAD LIFE.

THE BOY & THE NUTS

A boy put his hand into a pitcher, which was half full of nuts, and grasped just as many as his fingers could hold. But when he tried to take them out his hand caught in the narrow neck, and he began to cry. At this, his father said: Foolish boy! Take only half as much at one time:

GREED DEFEATS ITSELF.

THE CRAB AND HER MOTHER

Said an old Crab to her young one, Why do you walk crooked, child? walk straight! Mother, said the young crab, show me the way, will you? and when I see you walking straight, I will try to do the same.

PRACTICE WHAT YOU PREACH

THE LION AND HIS THREE COUNCILLORS

The lion called the donkey to ask her if his breath smelled; she said: Yes! so he bit off her head for a fool. Then he called the sheep, and asked him; the sheep said: No! so he tore him to pieces for a flatterer. At last he called the fox, and asked him. The fox said, looking at the remains of the donkey and the sheep: I am sorry, your majesty, but I have a bad cold, and cannot smell a thing!

A WISE MAN KEEPS SILENCE IN
THE REIGN OF A TYRANT

THE FLIES & THE HONEY POT

A pot of honey was upset in a grocer's shop, and a swarm of flies came to lap it up. It was so delicious that the flies waded in deeper and deeper, until they found themselves caught in the honey, and could not get away. What fools we are, said the flies then, To lose our lives for a moment's pleasure.

DO NOT LET ENJOYMENT LEAD YOU INTO
DANGER.

THE TWO POTS

Two pots, one of earthenware, the other of brass, were carried down a river together in a flood. The brass pot urged the earthen pot to keep by his side, for their mutual protection. Thank you for your offer, said the earthen pot, but that is just what I was afraid of; if you will only keep at a distance, I may float down in safety; but should we touch, I am sure to suffer.

AVOID POWERFUL NEIGHBOURS, FOR
IN A COLLISION, THE WEAKEST GOES DOWN.

THE SERPENT AND THE FILE

A serpent crawled into a blacksmith's shop for something to eat. The best he could find was a file, leave me alone fool! said the file: What chance have you against me, who can bite into the hardest steel?

TEST YOUR MEAT BEFORE YOU EAT.

THE WIDOW AND THE HEN

A widow had a plump hen who laid an egg every day, without fail. The widow thought to herself "If I give the hen twice as much barley, she will lay twice as many eggs. So she fed the hen twice a day. But after a few days the hen became so fat that she stopped laying eggs at all.

YOU CAN'T BRIBE NATURE

THE TWO WALLETS

Every man carries two wallets, one before and one behind, and both are full of faults. But one behind is full of his own. Thus it happens that men are blind to their own faults, but never lose sight of their neighbours'.

KNOW THYSELF!

THE LIONESS & HER CUB

Once there was great rivalry among the beasts, each one claiming to have the largest family. Finally the disputing beasts came to the Lioness, and said: Queen Lioness, how many children do you have at a birth? Only one growled the Lioness. But that one is a Lion!

QUALITY BEFORE QUANTITY

THE FIR-TREE & THE BRAMBLE

A fir-tree was one day boasting of itself to a bramble, and said: You are of no use at all; but how could barns and houses be built without me? Good sir, said the bramble Where the woodmen come here with their axes and saws, what would you give to be a bramble and not a fir.

HUMBLENESS IN SECURITY IS BETTER THAN LOFTINESS IN DANGER

10

THE SHEEP AND THE WOLF

A sheep, standing on the roof of a barn, saw a wolf passing below him. Ho there! you ugly wolf! he called. Get home! We don't want your kind of trash around this farm! Coward, said the wolf, Remember your words when we meet again on the pasture!

DO NOT BOAST IN THE PORT IF
YOU CANNOT FIGHT IN THE FIELD

THE FAWN & HER MOTHER

A fawn once said to her mother: Mother you are bigger than a dog, and swifter and better winded, and you have horns to defend yourself with; how is it that you are afraid of the hounds? The mother smiled and said, All this, my child, is true; but no sooner do I hear a dog bark, than, somehow or other, my heels take me off as fast as they can carry me.

YOU CANNOT ARGUE A COWARD INTO COURAGE.

THE TWO POTS

Two pots, one of earthenware, the other of brass, were carried down a river together in a flood. The brass pot urged the earthen pot to keep by his side, for their mutual protection. Thank you for your offer, said the earthen pot, but that is just what I was afraid of; if you will only keep at a distance, I may float down in safety; but should we touch, I am sure to suffer.

AVOID POWERFUL NEIGHBOURS, FOR
IN A COLLISION, THE WEAKEST GOES DOWN.

THE SERPENT AND THE FILE

A serpent crawled into a blacksmith's shop for something to eat. The best he could find was a file, leave me alone fool! said the file: What chance have you against me, who can bite into the hardest steel?

TEST YOUR MEAT BEFORE YOU EAT.

THE RAT & THE FROG

The rat went on a journey, and came to a river. There he saw a Frog, and said to her: Swim me across the river. The Frog didn't want to do this, but she was afraid of the rat, and said she would carry him across. He jumped on her back, and cried, Be off! and she started to swim. When they were half way across, the crafty Frog, stopped, and tried to shake the rat off into the water, so that he would. But as Fate would have, a hawk, seeing the commotion in the water swooped down and carried them both off.

KEEP TWO EYES OPEN: ONE FOR THE
DANGER AT HAND, ONE FOR THE DANGER
THAT MAY COME.

THE ROOSTER & THE DIAMOND

As a Rooster was scratching around in the straw of his barnyard for worms, he came upon a brilliant diamond that someone had lost there. All the Hens fluttered around to see it; but the Rooster went on with his scratching elsewhere. It's a fine thing for those who could use it, no doubt, he said, but as for me, I hope I can keep on finding corn and worms.

THE GREATEST JEWEL WILL NOT SATISFY HUNGER

THE CROW & THE PITCHER

A crow was dying of thirst, and could find no brook or pond. At last he came to a hut and outside it was a pitcher of water. But when he tried to drink the water, he couldn't reach down far enough. Then he tried to break the pitcher, but he wasn't strong enough. Finally he dropped small stones into the pitcher, one by one. At last the water rose high enough for him to quench his thirst.

NECESSITY IS THE MOTHER OF INVENTION

THE WIND & THE SUN

The wind and the sun once had an argument as to which was the stronger. They looked down on the earth and saw a traveller walking along the road, and decided to try their strength on him. The wind had the first trial: He blew and blew with all his might, and as cold to as he could. But the harder he blew, and the colder the wind the tighter the Traveller held his coat about him. When the Wind gave up the Sun had a try. It warmed the air, calmed the wind, and shone hotter and hotter until the Traveller had to take off his coat so the Sun won the contest.

PERSUASION IS OFTEN A STRONGER POWER THAN MERE FORCE

THE HARE AND HOUND

A hound having startled a hare from a bush, chased her for some distance, but the hare had the best of it, and off. A goatherd who was coming by jeered at the hound, saying that the hare was the better runner of the two. You forgot, replied the hound,

IT IS ONE THING TO BE RUNNING FOR
YOUR DINNER, AND ANOTHER FOR YOUR LIFE

THE DONKEY, THE FOX & THE LION

A donkey and a fox made a hunting alliance, and went out together to look for game. The fox was out in front, when he came upon a lion, who was also hunting. The fox seeing his danger, called softly to the lion: King lion, I have a donkey here that you can have; I will lead he lead you to him if you will let me go. The lion agreed, and no sooner had he killed the donkey, than he turned on the fox, and killed him too.

THOSE WHO DEAL WITH TRAITORS
ARE NOT TO BE TRUSTED

THE FOX & THE STORK

One day the Fox invited the Stork to dinner and for a joke had nothing served but soup in a shallow. The Fox could lap up the soup easily but the Stork could only wet the end of her long bill in it and so left the meal as hungry as when she came. I am so sorry, said the Fox, but that the soup is not seasoned to your taste! Do not apologize, said the Stork, but You must come and dine with me soon. So another day the fox came to dine with the Stork. Dinner was served in a long table in a jar with a narrow mouth and so only the Stork could eat it. Do not apologize for the Dinner said the Fox:

ONE BAD TURN DESERVES ANOTHER

THE MOUNTAIN IN LABOUR

Once a great mountain was rumbling and groaning and people came from far and wide to watch. It was said that that the mountain was going to give birth. Some said it would produce a hill; some said an ogre some said a monstrous animal. But after all the rumbling, groaning a shaking; the mountain laboured, and brought forth a mouse

GREAT PROMISES ARE NOT GREAT DEEDS

THE GOOSE WITH THE GOLDEN EGGS

Long ago a farmer had a magical goose, that laid a golden egg each day. Naturally, this goose was the wonder of the countryside, and all the farmers envied her rich owner. But once he had the taste of the gold, he could not get enough of it. Anxious to get the gold supply all at once, he killed the goose one night — only to find there was no gold inside at all.

ALWAYS PROTECT THE SOURCES OF YOUR GOOD FORTUNE

THE GOAT & THE VINE

A wild goat who was being chased by some hunters hid himself among the branches of a vine. The hunters passed without seeing him, but as soon as they were gone, he began to eat the thick branches that were covering him. Hearing the rustle of leaves, one of the hunters turned around, saw the head of the goat pulling at the vine, and shot the foolish animal after all.

DO NOT DESTROY YOUR PROTECTORS

THE WOLF IN SHEEP'S CLOTHING

Once a wolf who had trouble in catching sheep, decided to disguise himself. So he found the skin of a sheep, covered himself with it, and then mingled with the flock. By leading off lambs when the shepherd wasn't looking, the Wolf managed to feed himself very well every day; But one afternoon the shepherd wanted to prepare a feast for his family and looked for the fattest animal in the flock. His eye fell upon the Wolf in sheep's clothing, and he killed him on the spot.

EVERY DECEIT HAS ITS DANGERS

THE BEES & THE DRONES

The Bees had built their comb in a hollow tree, but some Drones took possession of it and claimed it for their own. The case was brought before the wise old Wasp, who agreed it was a difficult matter to decide. The only way to be sure who is was the owners, he said, was for each party to build a new comb, and whoever made the new comb look most like the one in dispute, were the real owners. The Bees agreed, but the Drones said no. Then the wise Wasp said: It is clear now who made the comb, and who cannot make it. It belongs to the Bees.

HONESTY NEVER FEARS TRIAL

THE ANT & THE GRASSHOPPER

One cold day in winter an Ant was dragging some corn he had buried in the summer. A Grasshopper, who was nearly starving, begged the Ant for a small bit of corn to save his life. What were you doing all last summer? asked the Ant. Oh, said the Grasshopper, I was very busy all summer long, singing. Well, said the Ant, Since you can sing all summer, you can dance all winter.

SAVE IN SUMMER; HAVE IN WINTER.

THE HARES & THE FROGS

The Hares were so frightened by other beasts that they did not know where to go. All the other animals seemed to pursue them, so they decided to put an end to all their fears and troubles by drowning themselves in the lake nearby. But just as the crowd of Hares came running to the lake, all the Frogs, in their turn frightened by the Hares, scuttled off into the water. Truly, said the leader of the Hares, things are not as bad as they seem.

THERE IS ALWAYS SOMEONE WORSE OFF THAN YOURSELF

THE LION, THE COW, THE GOAT & THE SHEEP

The cow, the goat and the sheep once went hunting with the lion, and after a long chase they caught a young deer. Then the animal was divided into 4 parts, one for each. Thereupon the lion said: I want you to know that the first part is mine because I am your king. The second part is mine because I am stronger than you are. The third part is mine because I run faster than you do. As for the fourth part: Let him who touches it beware, for he is my mortal enemy!

LET THE WEAK AVOID PARTNERSHIP
WITH THE STRONG

THE WOLF & THE SKULL

A wolf A wolf, going through a forest, found the skull of a man. He turned it over with his paw; but the skull said nothing. Ah, said the wolf: In times gone by you would have had something to say; in those days you were fat, and handsome; you could laugh, and sing, and drink and eat, and be merry; but now you are only an empty skull; and are good for nothing.

HEALTH AND MERRIMENT SOON DISAPPEAR;
ONLY THE WORKS OF MAN RETAIN. LIVE ON

THE COUNTRY MAID AND THE MILK JUG

A country maid was walking to the market with a full milk jug on her shoulder; and as she walked, she said to herself: With the money for this milk, I will buy myself some setting eggs; I will raise the chicks till they are big enough for market; and when I have sold them I will buy myself a beautiful green gown. With this green gown on I will look so beautiful that all the men will want to court me. But I will act proud, and shrug my shoulders so ...... and down crashed the jug and into a hundred pieces.

DON'T COUNT YOUR CHICKENS BEFORE
THE'RE THEY ARE HATCHED!

A ~~PIGEON WAS EXIT~~
A THIRSTY PIGEON

A pigeon was extremely thirsty, and had looked for water everywhere, in vain. At last she saw a glass of water painted on an inn sign; and without waiting to see it it was real she swooped down and dashed into the signboard, breaking her wing. The innkeeper took her in and cured her wing; but ~~who~~ she was a prisoner from that time on.

NEVER LET THIRST BETRAY YOUR ~~JUDGEMENT~~ JUDGEME

THE EAGLE & THE ARROW

A hunter ~~took~~ aim at an Eagle (with his arrow) and the arrow ~~sped true to the mark and~~ struck the Eagle in the heart. The noble bird fell to the ground, and as he fell, he saw that the arrow was winged with some of his own feathers Ah, said the dying Eagle, ...

HOW MUCH SHARPER ARE THE WOUNDS OF OUR OWN MAKING.

THE WOLF AND THE CRANE

A Wolf had a bone caught in his throat and ran through the forest in agony, begging every animal he met to help him, and promising a handsome reward. The Crane hearing of a reward, said she would help him. ~~and promising~~ She put her bill and neck down the Wolfs throat and drew out the bone. Then she asked for the reward. At this the Wolf bared his teeth and growled: Ungrateful creature! it is reward enough to put your head into a Wolfs paws and come out alive!

THOSE WHO HELP OTHERS FOR PROFITS, SHOULD BEWARE OF EVIL MEN.

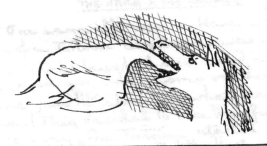

THE STAG AT THE POOL

One summer day a Stag came to a pool to drink, and saw himself reflected in the water. How beautiful and strong my antlers are, he said: But what a pity my legs are so thin and ugly! Just then he heard the baying of hounds. The legs he had been complaining of carried him swiftly from the hunters; but just as he thought he was safe, his beautiful horns caught in a thicket, and before he could get them free, the dogs were upon him.

USEFULNESS IS BETTER THAN BEAUTY

THE FARMER AND THE DOGS

One winter the snow was so deep for weeks on end that the farmer could not get out of his house and barn. Unable to get the food from outside he ate his own sheep; and when they were finished, had to eat his own goats. Still, the snow held, and the farmer killed & one of his own oxen. At this the dogs said one to another, it let us be off while we can; he has kept us for last only because he does not care for our meat.

WHEN YOUR NEIGHBOURS HOUSE IS
ON FIRE, LOOK TO YOUR OWN

THE HARE & THE TORTOISE

One warm afternoon a Hare was making fun of a Tortoise because he was so slow. The Tortoise laughed and said he could beat the Hare any day. Come on then said the Hare, and I'll show you what kind of runner I am! They decided to race to a forest, a mile or so away. The Tortoise started off at once, at his steady pace. But the Hare said boastfully, I think I'll take a little nap first, I've plenty of time to spare. But when the Hare woke up the sun was setting in the west, and though he raced to the edge of the forest as fast as he could go, he found the Tortoise there before him.

SLOW AND STEADY WINS THE RACE.

THE WAGONER & HERCULES.

A farmer was driving his wagon carelessly along a muddy road, when the wheels sank into the soft clay, and the horses came to a standstill. Whipping and shouting at the horses did no good: The wagon would not budge. Then the farmer climbed into the back of the wagon, and kneeled down to pray to Hercules: Good god Hercules, help me now with your great strength! But Hercules looked down, and said: My good man, first put your own shoulder to the wheel:

THE GODS HELP THOSE WHO HELP THEMSELVES

THE DONKEY IN OFFICE

One day a donkey was loaned to a priest by his master, to carry a religious image in a procession. As the Donkey marched through the town; he saw all the people bowing in reverence, and this made him so proud — for he thought they were bowing to him — and he decided he would not be driven anymore. But the minute he stopped, his driver whipped him on again saying: "you silly donkey, it is not you all the people are now bowing to, but the sacred image you are carrying."

FOOLS TAKE TO THEMSELVES THE RESPECT THAT IS SHOWN TO THEIR OFFICE

THE BUNDLE OF STICKS

A farmer was worried because his sons were always quarrelling, so finally he said to them: Go and gather me a bundle of sticks. After some quarrelling the two youngest got the sticks. The Farmer then tied the bundle with a strong cord, and said: Now break this bundle! But they couldn't: Now break them seperately, and they did this easily.

Let this be a lesson to you, said the Farther that you must stop quarrelling and work together, for

IN UNION THERE IS STRENGTH

THE WOLF AND THE SHEPHERD

A crafty Wolf had for a long time hung about a flock of sheep and done them no harm. He pretended that he was reformed, and acted like a sheepdog. After a while the shepherd, who had begun by fearing him, looked upon him as a helper; and one day even went into town, thinking that the Wolf would guard his flock from any danger. But of course this was just the opportunity the Wolf had been waiting for, and while the Shepherd was away, the entire flock was killed.

BEWARE OF VILLAINS WHO ACT LIKE FRIENDS

THE THIEF AND THE DOG.

Once a thief thought he was very clever. He used to boast to his friends that no lock could keep him out, and no dog could frighten him. One night he came to rob a farmer's house; but the dog saw him and started to bark. There, there! Good doggie! said the thief, and threw the dog a fine piece of meat. At this the faithful dog barked loud at them even For, said he to the thief: I was suspicious of you at first, but now I know you are up to no good whatsoever!

HONEYED WORDS AND A BRIBE PRECEDE VILLAINY.

THE MICE IN COUNCIL

The mice were desperate because of a cat, who caught one or two of them every night. So they called a council, to decide how best to put an end to their troubles. Many plans were suggested and discarded; but at last a smart young mouse spoke up and said: Why not put a bell on the cat, so that we can hear her coming? Everybody thought it was the best idea, and a vote was just about to be taken when a shrewd old mouse, who had kept quiet until then, remarked: Who will put the bell on the cat?

IT IS ONE THING TO MAKE GREAT PLANS;
AND ANOTHER TO CARRY THEM OUT.

THE CREAKING WHEELS

Some Oxen were dragging a heavy wagon along the road, and the wheels of the wagon were creaking mightily. Fool of a wagon! said the driver, why to you creak and complain, when those who are pulling the weight do not complain

THOSE WHO CRY LOUDEST ARE NOT ALWAYS THE
MOST HURT

THE WOLF AND THE GOAT

A Wolf, seeing a fat Goat feeding at the edge of a high cliff, begged her to come down lower, for fear he said, that she might miss her footing and be hurt. And anyway, he added: The grass is really much sweeter and greener down here. To which the Goat replied; Is it to my dinner you invite me, or your own?

WHEN A VILLAIN SMILES, HE BAITS HIS TRAP.

THE BOY WHO CRIED "WOLF" TOO OFTEN.

A boy who thought that his life as an shepherd was boring, and so he one day he shouted to the neighbouring farmer : Help! There is a Wolf among my sheep! Help! Help! The Farmer and several other people rushed to his help, and he laughingly told them; It was only a joke. The next day the Boy heard a low growl, he turned round and saw a Wolf among his flock, killing them. Help! cried the unfortunate boy! There is a Wolf among my flock. But Everybody said : Oh he is only joking, he's probably trying to pull our legs again, so nobody came to help him and the whole flock was killed.

NEVER TRY THE A JOKE ONCE & WHEN IT HAPPENS EXPECT PEOPLE TO BELIEVE YOU.

PART 2.

Old fables. Written in the 18th cent.
In the original style of our language

THE SPIDER AND THE SILKWORM

How vainly we promise ourselves, that our flimsy productions will be rewarded with immortal honour! A spider, busied in spreading from one side of a room to the other, was asked by an industrious silkworm, to what end he spent so much time, and so much labour in making such a number of lines and ill circles? The spider angrily replied, do not disturb me, thou ignorant thing. I transmit my ingenuity to my posterity, and fame is the object of my wishes. Just as he had spoken, a chambermaid, coming into the room to feed the silkworms, saw the spider at his work, and with one stroke of her broom, and destroyed at once his labours, and his hopes of fame.

> HE THAT IS EMPLOYED IN THE WORKS OF USE
> GENERALLY ADVANTAGES HIMSELF OF OTHERS;
> WHILE HE WHO TOILS ALONE FOR FAME
> MUST OFTEN EXPECT TO LOSE HIS LABOUR

THE MOCK BIRD

There is a certain bird in the West Indies, which has a faculty of mimicking the notes of every other songster, without being able himself to add any original original strains himself to the concert. As one of these Mock-birds was displaying his talent of ridicule among the branches of a venerable wood: 'Tis very well, said a little warbler, speaking in the name of the rest, we grant that our music is not without its faults: but why will you not favour us with a strain of your own?

RIDICULE APPEARS WITH A VERY BAD GRACE,
IN PERSONS WHO POSSESS NO ONE TALENT BESIDE.

THE BOY AND THE NETTLE.

A little boy playing in the fields, chanced to be stung by a nettle, and came crying to his father: he told him, it had been hurt by this nasty weed several times before; and that he was always afraid of it.

THE BOY AND THE NETTLE

A little boy playing in the fields chanced to be stung by a nettle and came crying to his father: he told him, he had been hurt by this nasty weed several times before; and that he was afraid of it; and that now he did but touch it, as lightly as possible, and he was severely stung. Child, says he, your touching the nettle so gently and so timourously is the very reason of its hurting you. A nettle may be handled safely, if you do it with courage and resolution. If you seize it boldly and grip it fast, be assured it will never sting you. And you will meet many persons as well as things in the world, which ought to be treated in the very same manner.

THERE ARE CERTAIN PERSONS WHO REQUIRE TO BE
TREATED WITH SPIRIT AND RESOLUTION RATHER THAN
EITHER TENDERNESS OR DELICACY.

THE FOX AND THE BRAMBLE

A fox was closely pursued by a pack of dogs, took shelter under the covert of a bramble. He rejoiced in this asylum, and for a while was very happy; but soon found that if he attempted to stir he was wounded by the thorns and prickles on every side. However, making a virtue of necessity, he forbore to complain; he comforted himself with reflecting, that no bliss is perfect; that good are mixed with evil, and flow from the same fountain. These briars indeed, said he, will tear my skin a little, yet they keep off the dogs. For the sake of good, then, let me bear evil with patience. Each bitter has its sweet; and these brambles, though they wound my flesh, preserve my life from danger.

> WE SHOULD BEAR WITH PATIENCE A SMALL EVIL,
> WHEN IT IS CONNECTED WITH A GREATER GOOD

JUPITER AND THE HERDSMAN

A herdsman missed a young heifer out of his grounds, and after having diligently sought for it in vain, when he could by no other means gain intelligence of it, betook himself at last to his prayers. Great Jupiter, said he, shew me but the villain who has done me this injury, and I will give thee in sacrifice the fattest kid from my flock. He no sooner uttered his petition, than turning the corner of a wood, he was struck with the sight of a monstrous lion, preying on the carcass of his heifer. Trembling and pale, O Jupiter, cried he, I offer thee a kid if thou would grant my petition; I now offer thee a bull if thou wilt deliver me from the consequence of it.

> WERE OUR ILL JUDGED PRAYERS TO BE ALWAYS GRANTED,
> HOW MANY WOULD BE RUINED AT THEIR OWN REQUEST!

THE OWL AND THE NIGHTINGALE

A formal solemn spoken owl had many years made his habitation in a grove amongst the ruins of an old monastery, and had pored so often on some mouldy manuscripts, the stupid relics of a monkish library, that he grew infected with the pride and pedantry of the place, and mistaking gravity for wisdom, would sit whole days with his eyes half shut, fancying himself profoundly learned. It happened, as he sat one evening, half buried in meditation, and half asleep, that a nightingale, unluckily perching near him, began her melodious lays. He started from his reverie and with a horrid screech interrupted her song.

— Be gone, cried he, thou impertinent minstrel, nor distract with thy noisy dissonance my sublime contemplations; and know, vain songster, that harmony consists in truth alone, which please by laborious study alone; and not in languishing notes, fit only to sooth the ear of a love-sick maid. Conceited pedant returned the nightingale, whose wisdom lies only in the feathers that muffle up thy face, unmeaning face; music is a natural and rational entertainment, and though not adapted to the ears of an owl, has been relished and admired by all who are possessed of true taste and elegance.

'TIS NATURAL FOR A PEDANT TO DESPISE THOSE ARTS
WHICH POLISH OUR MANNERS AND WOULD EXTIRPATE
PEDANTRY

THE COUNTRYMAN AND THE SNAKE.

An honest countryman deserved a snake lying under a hedge, almost frozen to death. He was moved with compassion; and bringing it home, he laid it near the fire and gave it some new milk. Thus fed and nourished cherished, the creature presently began to revive, but no sooner had it recovered strength enough to do mischief, than he sprang on the country mans wife, bit one of his children, and, in short, threw the whole family into confusion and terror. Ungrateful wretch! cried the man, thou hast sufficient taught me how ill-judged it is to confer benefits on the worthless and undeserving. So saying he snatched up an hatchet, and cut the snake in pieces.

TO CONFER EITHER POWER UPON THE MISCHIEVOUS OR FAVOURS ON THE UNDESERVING, IS A MISAPPLICATION OF OUR BENEVOLENCE.

THE DOG AND THE SHADOW

An hungry Spaniel, having stolen a piece of flesh from a butcher's shop, was carrying it across a river. The water being clear and the sun shining brightly, he saw his own image in the stream, and it to be another dog with a more delicious morsel; upon which, unjustly and greedily opening his jaws to snatch at the shadow, he lost the substance.

AN OVER-GREEDY DISPOSITION OFTEN SUBJECTS US TO 'LOSE' WHAT WE ALREADY POSSESS.

THE OLD MAN AND DEATH

An old man, quite spent with carrying a burthen of sticks which with much labour he had gathered in the wood, called upon Death to release him from the fatigues he had endured. Death hearing the invocation, was immediately at his elbow, and asked him what he wanted, frighted and trembling at his sudden appearance; — O good sir! said he, my burthen had like to have slipt from me, and being unable to recover it myself, I only implored your assistance to replace it on my shoulders.

MEN UNDER CALAMITY MAY SEEM TO WISH
FOR DEATH, BUT THEY SELDOM BID HIM WELCOME
WHEN HE STARES THEM IN THE FACE.

THE SNAKE AND THE HEDGEHOG

By intreaties of a Hedgehog half starved with cold, a Snake was once perswaded persuaded to recieve him into her cell. He no sooner entered into her cell than his prickles began to be very uneasy to his companion: upon which the Snake desired he would provide himself another lodging, as she found upon trial that the apartment would not accommodate both. Nay, said the Hedgehog, let them that are uneasy in their situation exchange it; for my own part, I am very well contented where I am; if you are not you are welcome to remove when ever you think proper.

'TIS EVER IMPORTANT IMPRUDENT TO JOIN INTERESTS
WITH THOSE WHO ARE ABLE TO IMPOSE UPON US
THEIR OWN CONDITIONS.

Part 3.   Fables by James Thurber
In American Lingo!

THE FATHER AND HIS DAUGHTER

A little girl had so many picture books given to her for her birthday that her father, who have run his office and let her mother run the home, thought his daughter should give one or two of her new books to a little neighbour boy called Robert who had dropped in, more by design than by chance. Now, taking books or anything else, from a little girl is like taking books from an arab, or candy from a baby, but the father of the little girl had his way and Robert got two of her books. "After all, that leaves you with nine," said the father, who thought he was a philosopher or a child psychologist, and couldn't shut his big fatuous mouth on the subject.

A few weeks later, the father went to his library to look up "Father" in the Oxford English Dictionary, to feast his eyes on the praise of fatherhood through the centuries, but he couldn't find the volume F–G, and then he discovered that the other three were missing too— A—B, L—M and V—Z. He began to probe his household, and soon learned what had become of them. "A man came to the door this morning," said his little daughter, "And he didn't know how to get from here to Torrington or from Torrington to Winstead, and he was a nice man, much nicer than Robert, and so I gave him four of your books. After all there are thirteen volumes in the English Dictionary, and that leaves you Nine."

THIS TRUTH HAS BEEN KNOWN FROM HERE TO MENANDER,
SAUCE FOR THE GOSLING'S NOT SAUCE FOR THE GANDER

THE GODFATHER AND HIS GODCHILD.

A worldly wise collector, who had trotted the globe collecting everything he could shoot, or buy, or make off with, and called upon his godchild, a little girl of five, after a year of collecting in various countries of the world.

"I want to give you three things," he said. "Any three things your heart desires. I have diamonds in Africa, and a rhinoceros horn, scarabs from Egypt, emeralds from Guatemala, chessmen of ivory and moose's antlers, signal drums, ceremonial gongs, temple bells, and three rare and remarkable dolls. "Now tell me," he concluded, patted the little girl on the head; "what do you want more than anything else in the world?"

His little godchild, who was not a hesitater, did not hesitate. "I want to break your glasses and spit on your shoes." she said.

THOUGH STATICIANS IN OUR TIME HAVE NEVER KEPT THE SCORE,
MAN WANTS A GREAT DEAL HERE BELOW AND WOMAN EVEN MORE.

THE WOLF AND AT THE DOOR

Mr. and Mrs. Sheep were sitting in their sitting room with their daughter, who was as pretty as she was edible, when there was at the door "It's a gentleman caller," said the daughter.

"It's the fuller brushman," said her mother. The cautious father got up and ~~to~~ looked out of the window. "It's the Wolf," he said. "I can see his tail."

"Don't be silly" said the mother. "It's the fuller brush man, and that's his brush." And she went to the door and opened it, and the wolf came in and ran away with the daughter.

"You were right, after all," admitted the mother, sheepishly.

MOTHER DOES NOT~~E~~ *ALWAYS* KNOW BEST.

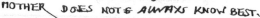

THE WORM AND THE WEAVER.

A weaver watched in wide-eyed wonder a silkworm spinning its cocoon in a wh white mulberry tree.

"Where do you get that stuff?" asked the admiring weaver.

"Do you want to make something out of it?" inquired the silkworm, eagerly.

Then the weaver and the silkworm went their seperate ways, for each thought the other had insulted him. We live, man and worm, in a time when time almost everything can mean almost anything, for this is the age of gobbledy dook, doubletalk and bunda.

> A WORD TO THE WISE IS NOT SUFFICIENT
> IF IT DOESN'T MAKE ANY SENSE.

THE BUTTERFLY, THE LADYBUG AND THE PHOEBE.

A phoebe, bugwinner for a nestful of fledgelings, flew out one day to provide dinner for his family, and came upon a ladybug in frantic flight. "I know you can catch anything smaller than sound," said ladybug, "for you are the fastest of flycatchers, but my house is on fire and my children will burn unless I fly away home."

The Phoebe, who had sometimes been guilty of wishing this his own house were on fire, let the ladybug fly away, and turned his attention to a beautiful butterfly, "Is your house on fire and will your children burn?" The phoebe asked. "Nothing so mundane as that," said the Butterfly. "I have no children and I have no house, for I am an angel, as anyone can see." She fluttered her wings at the world about her. "This is heaven," she said.

"This is heaven," cried the fledgelings as they devoured the Butterfly for desert that night.

> SHE WHO GOES UNARMED IN PARADISE SHOULD BE
> SURE THAT'S REALLY WHERE SHE IS.

VARIATIONS ON THE FABLE "THE FOX AND THE CROW"

I.

A fox, attracted by the scent of something
followed his nose to a tree in which sat a
crow with a piece of cheese in his beak.
"Oh, cheese," said the Fox scornfully, "That's for
mice."

The crow removed the removed the cheese with
his talons and said, "You always hate the thing
you cannot have, as for instance grapes."
"Grapes are for birds." said the fox haughtily.
"I am an epicure, a gourmet, and a gastronome."

The embarassed crow, ashamed to be seen
eating mouse food by a great specialist in dining,
hastily dropped the cheese. The fox caught it
deftly, swallowed it with relish, and said "Merci",
politely, and trotted away.

II

This time the Fox, who determined not t
A fox had used all his blandishments in vain,
for all he could not flatter the crow in the tree
and make him drop the cheese he held in his beak.
Suddenly, the crow tossed the cheese to the astonish-
ed fox. Just then the Farmers, from whose kitchen
the loot had been stolen, appeared, carrying a rifle,
looking for the robber. The fox turned and ran
for the woods.

"There goes the guilty son of a vixen now!" cried
the crow, who, in case you do not happen to know it,
can see the glint of a gun barrel at a greater
distance than anybody.

IV

In the great and ancient tradition, the crow in the tree with the cheese in his beak began singing, and the cheese fell into the fox's lap.

"You sing like a shovel," said the fox, with a grin, but the crow pretended not to hear and cried out, "Quick give me back the cheese! here comes the farmer with his rifle!"

"Why should I give you back your cheese?" the wily fox demanded.

"Because the farmer has a gun, and I can fly faster than you can run."

So the frightened fox tossed back the cheese to the crow, who ate it, and said, "Dearie me, my eyes are playing tricks on me — or am I playing tricks on you? Which do you think?" But there was no reply because the fox had slunk away into the woods.

Book ~~Three~~ Two.

Selected poems.

<u>Part 1</u> <u>Sea and Adventure</u>.

<u>THE MIDNIGHT SKATERS</u>

The hop-poles stand in cones,
The icy ponds lurks under,
The pole-tops steeple to the thorns
Of stars, sounds gulfs of wonder;
But not the tallest there, 'tis said,
Could fathom to this pond's black bed.

Then is not death at watch
Within those secret waters?
What wants he but to catch
Earth's heedless sons and daughters?
With but a crystal parapet
Between, he has his engines set.

Then on blood shouts, on, on,
Twirl, wheel and whip above him,
Dance on this ball floor thin and
wan,
Use him as though you love him;
Court him, elude him, reel and pass,
And ℔ let him hate you through the
glass.

EDMUND BLUNDEN. (6.189

FOG.

Over the oily swell it heaved, it rolled,
Like some foul creature, filmy, nebulous.
It pushed out streaming tentacles, took
Clammy and cold, blotted the sun,
Crept round and over us.

Day long, night long, it hid us from the sky
— Hid us from sun and stars as in a
Tomb. Shrouded in mist a berg went
Groaning by. Far and forlorn we heard the
Blinds ships cry. Like Lost souls wailing in
a hopeless gloom.

Like a bell-weather clanging from a
fold, a codder her dories. With scared
breath the steamer sirens shrieked;
and mad bells tolled.

Through time eternal in the dark we
rolled played a game of blind man's buff
with Death.

CROSBIE GARSTIN (1887-1930)

SIR PATRICK SPENS

I. the sailing.

The King sits in Dunfermline town
Drinking the blude-red wine;
'O where will I get a skeely shipper
To sail this new ship o' mine?'

O up and spake an eldern knight,
Sat at the king's right knee:
'Sir Patrick Spens is the best sailor
That ever sailed the sea.'

Our king has written a broad letter,
And sealed it with his hand,
And sent it to Sir Patrick Spens,
Was walking on the strand.

'To Noroway, to Norowgy,
To Norowgy o'er the foam;
The king's daughter o' Norowgy,
'Tis thou must bring her home.'

The first word that Sir Patrick read
So loud, loud laugh'd he;
The next word that Sir Patrick read
The tear blinded his e'e.

'O who is this has done this deed
And told the king o' me, to send us out,
At this time o' year, to sail the
The sea?

Be it rain, be it wet, be it hail,
Be it sleet our ship must sail the
foam; The king's daughter o' Norway
'Tis we must fetch her home.'

They hoisted their sails on Monenday
Morn with all the speed they may;
They have landed in Noroway
Upon a Wednesday.

II

The Return.

THE MEN OF NOROWAY SEEM TO HAVE
INSULTED THEIR SCOTTISH GUESTS BY
HINTTING THAT THEY WERE STAYING TOO
LONG, AND THIS CAUSED SIR PATRICK
SPENS TO SAIL FOR HOME WAITING FOR FAIR
WEATHER.

Make ready, make ready, my merry
men all! Our good ship sails the morn."
— 'Now ever alack, my master dear,
I fear a deadly storm.

I saw the new moon late yast'r-e'en
With the old moon in her arm;
And with go to sea, master,
I fear we'll come to harm.'

They had not sailed a league, a
league, a league but barely three,
When the lift grew dark, and the
wind blew loud, and gurly grew the sea.

The anchors brake, and the topmost
Cap, It was such a deadly storm;
And the waves came o'er the broken
Ship till all her sides were torn.

'O where will I get a good sailor
  To take my helm in hand,
While I go up to the tall top mast
  To see if I can spy land?'——

He had not gone a step, a step,
A step, a step but barely one,
When a bolt flew flew out of our
Goodly ship, and the salt sea it came in.

Go fetch a web o' the silken cloth,
  Another o' the twine,
And wap them into our ship's side,
  And let not the sea come in.

They fetch'd a web o' the silken cloth,
Another o' the twine,
And they wapp'd them round the good ship's
Side, but still the sea came in.

SECTION II.
GENERAL.

The ship of Rio.

There was a ship of Rio
Sailed out into the Blue,
And nine and ninety monkeys
Were all her jovial crew.
From bosun to the cabin boy,
From quarter to caboose,
There wasn't a stick stitch of
Calico to breech 'em — tight or
Loose ; From spar to deck, from
Deck to keel, from barnacle to
Shroud, There weren't a pair
Of reach-me-downs to all that
Jabbering crowd. But wasn't
It a gladsome sight,
When round the deep sea gales,
To see them reef her for' and aft,
A-swinging by their tails!
O, wasn't it a gladsome sight,
When glassy calm did come,
To see them squatting tailor-wise
Around a keg of Rum! Oh wasn't
It a gladsome sight, When in
She sailed to land, To see them
All a-scampering skip for
Nuts across the sand!

WALTER DE LA MARE.

EXTRACTS FROM HORATIUS.

Lars Porsena of Clusium
  By the nine gods he swore
That the great house of Tarquin
  Should suffer wrong no more.
By the nine gods he swore it,
  And named the trysting day,
And bade his messengers ride forth
  To summ East, West, South and North
To summon his array.

And now hath every city
Sent up her tale of men
The foot are fourscore thousand
The horse are thousands ten.
Before the gates of Sutrium
Is met the great array.
A proud man is Lars Porsena
Upon this trysting day.

But by the yellow Tiber
　　Was tumult and affright:
From all the spacious champaign
　　To Rome men took their flight.
A mile round the city
　　The throng stopped up the ways;
A fearful sight it was to see
　　Through two long nights and days.

For aged folk on crutches,
　　And women great with child,
And mothers sobbing over babes
　　That clung to them and smiled,
And sick men borne in litters
　　High on the necks of slaves,
And troops of sun-burned husbandmen
　　With reaping-hooks and staves,

And droves of mules and asses
  Laden with skins of wine,
And endless flock of goats and sheep,
  And endless herds of kine,
And endless trains of waggons
  That creaked beneath the weight
Of corn-sacks and of household goods,
  Choked every roaring gate.

They held a council standing
  Before the River-gate;
Short time was there, yore well may
  Guess, for musing or debate.
Out spake the consul roundly:
  'The bridge must straight go down;
For, since Janiculum is lost,
  Nought else can save the town.'

And nearer fast and nearer
  Doth the red whirlwind come;
And louder still and still more loud,
  From underneath that rolling cloud
Is heard the trumpet's war note-proud,
  The trampling, and the hum.
And plainly and more plainly
  Now through the gloom appears,
Far to the left, far to the right,
  In broken gleams of dark-blue light,
The long array of helmets bright,
  The long array of spears.

But the Consul's brow was sad,
   And the Consul's speech was low,
And darkly looked he at the wall,
   And darkly at the foe.
"Their van will be upon us
   Before the bridge goes down;
And if they once may win the
   Bridge, what hope to save the town?"

Then out spoke brave Horatius,
   The captain of the gate:
"To every man upon this earth
   Death cometh soon or late:
And how can man die better
   Than facing fearful odds
~~And~~ For the ashes of his fathers
And the temples of his gods?

Hew down the bridge, Sir Consul,
  With all the speed ye may;
I, with to more to help me,
  Will hold the foe in play.
In yon strait path a thousand
  May well be stopped by three.
Now who will stand on either hand
  And keep the bridge with me?"

HORATIUS

But harke the cry is Astur
And loe! The ranks divide ;
    And the great Lord of Luna
Comes with his stately stride .
    Upon his angle shoulders
Clangs loud the fourfold shield,
    And in his hand he shakes the brand
Which none but he can wield .

Then whirling up his broadsword
　　With both hands to the height,
He pushed against Horatius,
　　And smote with all his might.
With shield and blade Horatius
　　Right deftly turned the blow.
The blow though turned, came yet
　　Too nigh; It missed his helm,
But gashed his thigh: The Tuscans
　　Raised a joyful cry to see
The red blood flow.

But all Etruria's noblest
    Felt their ~~heavsh~~ hearts sink to see
On the earth the bloody corpses,
    In the path of the dauntless three :
And, from the ghastly entrance,
    Where those bold Romans stood,
All shrank, like boys who unaware,
Ranging the woods to start a hare,
Come to the mouth of the dark lair
Where, growling low, a fierce old bear
    Lies amidst bones and blood.

Was none, who would be foremost
    To lead such dire attack :
But those behind cried "Forward!"
    And those before cried, "Back."
And backward now and forward
    Wavers the deep array;
And on the tossing sea of steel,
    To and fro the standards reel;
And the victorious trumpet-peal
    Dies fitfully away.

But meanwhile axe and lever
 Have manfully been plied;
And now the bridge hangs tottering
 Above the boiling tide.
'Come back, come back, Horatius!'
 Loud cried the fathers all.
'Back, Lartius! back, Herminius!
 Back, ere the ruin fall!'

Back darted Spurius Lartius;
 Herminius darted back:
And as they passed, beneath their
 Feet they felt the timbers crack.

Alone stood brave Horatius,
　　But constant still in mind;
Thrice thirty thousand foes before,
　　And the broad flood behind.

'O Tiber! Father Tiber!
　　To whom the Romans pray,
A Roman's life, a Roman's arms,
　　Take thou in charge ~~to-day~~ this day!'
So he spake, and speaking sheathed
　　The good sword by his side,
And with his harness on his back
　　Plunged headlong in the tide.

No sound of joy or sorrow
　　Was heard from either bank;
But friends and foes in dumb surprise,
　　With parted lips and straining eyes,
Stood gazing where sank;
And when above the surges they saw
His crest appear, all Rome sent
　　forth a rapturous cry,
And even the ranks of Tuscany
　　Could scarce forbear to cheer.

Never, I ween, did swimmer,
   In such an evil case,
Struggle through such a raging flood
   Safe to the landing-place:
But his limbs were borne up bravely
   By the brave heart within,
And our good father within, Tiber
   Bare bravely up his chin.

And now he feels the bottom;
   Now on dry earth he stands;
~~Now on dry earth he stands;~~
Now round him throng the Fathers
   To press his gory hands;
And now with shouts and clapping,
   And noise of weeping loud,
He enters through the river-gate
   Borne by the joyous crowd.

They gave him of the corn-land,
    That was of public right,
As much as two strong oxen
    Could plough from morn till night;
And they made a molten image,
    ~~And there it stands unto this day~~
    And set it up on high
And there it stands unto this day
    To witness if I lie.

It stands in the Comitium
    Plain for all folk to see;
Horatius in his harness,
    Halting upon one knee :
And underneath is written,
    In letters all of gold,
How valiantly he kept the bridge
    In the brave days of old.

HOC EST HORATIUS SERVAVIT
PONTEM

THE END.

Lord Macaulay

EPITAPHS

FROM A TOMBSTONE IN SUTTON PARISH CHURCHYARD

Here lies a man who was killed by
Lightening; he died when prospects
Seemed to be brightening. He might
Have cut a flash in this world of trouble,
But the flash cut him, and he lies
In the stubble.

$

Here lies my poor wife,
Without bed or blanket,
But dead as a door-nail
And be thankit.

EPITAPH FROM AUSTRALIA.

God took our flower - our little Nell
He thought he too would like a smell.

EPITAPH ON A SHREW.

Here lies thank Heaven
A woman who
Quarrelled and stormed
Her whole life through
Tread lightly o'er her slumbering form
For fear you wake another storm.

ARABELLA YOUNG

Beneath this stone
. A lump of clay
Lies Arabella Young
   Who on the 21st of May
   1771
Began to hold her ~~young~~ tongue.

FREDERICK TWITCHELL
   Departed June 11, 1811
   Aged 24 years, 5 mos.
Here lies the bones of Lazy Fred
Who wasted precious time in bed
Some plaster down on his head
      And thanks be praised—
      Our Freddie's dead.

SOME PSEUDO - EPITAPHS

Here lies I and my three daughters
Killed by drinking Cheltenham waters.
If we'd kept to Epsom Salts.
We wouldn't be lying in these 'ere vaults.

Solomon Isaac's lies ~~underground~~ in
This ground.
Don't jingle money when walking around.

Here lies a mother of twenty-eight.
It might have been more, but now it's too
late.

EPITAPH ON HIMSELF.

I was buried near this dyke,
That my friends may weep as much as
They like.
WILLIAM BLAKE.

EPITAPH ON A PARSON.

Here lies the reverend Jonathan Doe,
Where he's gone to I don't know.
If haply to the realms above,
Farewell to happiness and love.
If haply to a lower level,
I can't congratulate the Devil.

LIMERICK – EPITAPH

There was an old man who averred
He had learned how to fly like a bird.
Cheered by thousands of people
He leapt from the steeple———
This tomb states the date it occurred.

ON DOCTOR . ISAAC LETSOME

When's people's ill they comes to I,
I physics, bleeds, and sweats 'em,
Sometimes they live, sometimes they die;
What's that to I ? I Letsome.

AT LEEDS

Here lies my wife
He lies she;
Hallelujah!
Hallelujee!

EPITAPH ON A DYER AT LINCOLN

Here lies John Hyde;
He first lived, and then he died;
He dyed to live, and liv'd to dye,
And hopes to live eternally.

John Bun.

Here lies John Bun,
He was killed by a gun,
His name was not Bun, but Wood, but
Wood would not rhyme with Gun,
but Bun would.

THE SHADES OF NIGHT.

The shades of night were falling fast
And the rain was falling faster
When through an Alpine village passed
An Alpine village pastor.

A.E. HOUSEMAN.

THE OPTIMIST AND THE PESSIMIST.

The optimist, who always was a fool,
Cries, 'Look! My mug of ale is still
Half full!'
His brother gives the facts their proper twist—
'My mug's half empty!' sighs the pessimist.

ARNOLD SILCOCK.

COCKNEY RHYMES

EPITAPH ON A 'MARF'

Wot a marf 'e'd got,
Wot a marf.
Where 'e wos a kid,
Goo' lor' luv'll
'Is poor muvver
Musta 'a' fed 'im wiv a shuvvle.

Wot a gap 'e'd got,
Pore chap,
'E'd never been known to laf,
'Cos if 'e did
It's a penney to a quid
'E'd a' split 'is fice in 'arf.

TRADITIONAL.

Yawcob Strauss.

I have I haf von funny leedle poy,
Vot gomes schust to mine knee;
Der queerest schap, der createst rogue,
As efer you dit see.
He runs, und schumps, und smas schmashes
Dings in all barts of der house;
But vot off dat? he vas mine son,
Mine leedle Yawcob Strauss.

He get der measles und der mumbs,
Und eferyding dot's oudt;
He sbills mine glass of lager bier,
Poots schnuff indo mine kraut.
He fills mine pipe mit limberg cheese—
Dot vas der roughest chouse;
I'd dake dot vrom no oder poy
But leedle Yawcob Strauss.

83.

He dakes der milk-ban for a dhrum,
And cuts mine cane in dwo,
To makes der schticks to beat it mit—
Mine goodness, dot vos drue!
I dinks mine hed was schplit abart,
He kicks oup sooch a touse:
But never mind; der poys was few
Like dot young Yawcob Strauss.

He asks me questions, sooch as dese:
Who baints mine nose so red?
Who vas it cuts dot schmoothth blace oudt
Vrom der hair upon mine hed?
Und where der blaze goes vrom der
Lamp vene'er der glim I douse,
How gan I all dose dings eggsblain
To dot schmall Yawcob Strauss.

I somedimes dinke I schall go wild
Mit sooch a grazy poy;
Und vish vonce more I gould haf rest,
Und beaceful dimes enshoy;
But ven he vash asleep in ped,
So quiet as a mouse,
I prays der Lord, "Dake anyding,
But leave dot Yawcob Strauss?

THE END.

Charles Follen Adams.

ORTHUTPH.

A silly young fellow named Hyde
In a funeral procession was spied;
When asked, "Who is dead?"
He giggled and said,
"I don't know; I just came for the ride."

ANON.

~~THE DIVERTING H~~

THE EAGLE.

He clasps the crag with crooked hands;
Close to the sun in lonely lands,
Ring'd with the azure ~~world~~, he stands.

The wrinkled sea beneath him crawls;
He watches from his mountain walls,
And b like a thunderbolt he falls.

LORD TENNYSON.

YE MARINERS OF ENGLAND.

Ye mariners of England
That guard our native seas,
Whose flag has braved, a thousand
Years, the battle and the breeze,—
Your glorious standard launch
Again to match another foe!
And sweep through the deep,
While the stormy winds do blow,—
While the battle rages loud and long,
And the stormy winds do blow.

The spirits of your fathers
Shall start from every wave!
For deck it was their field of fame,
And Ocean was their grave.
Where Blake and mighty Nelson fell
Your manly hearts shall glow,
As ye sweep through the deep,
While the stormy winds do blow,—
While the battle rages loud and long
And the stormy winds do blow.

Brittannia needs no bulwarks,
No towers along the steep;
Her march is over the mountain waves,
Her home is on the deep.
With thunder from her native oak
She quells the floods below,
As they roar on the shore
When the stormy winds do blow, —
While When the battle rages loud
And long, and the stormy winds do
Blow.

The meteor Flag of England
Shall yet terrific burn,
Till danger's troubled night depart
And the star of peace return:
Then, then ye ocean-warriors!
Our song and feast shall flow
To the fame of your name,
When the storm has ceased to blow,—
When the fiery fight is heard no
More, and the storm has ceased to blow.

THE END.

Thomas Campbell.

The Author

Born Bromley Kent, November 1948, Nicholas James Philip Wegner, (Nicholas Philip James from 2002), studied painting with Frank Auerbach and Keith Vaughan at the Slade School of Art UCL, and History of Art (MA) at Kingston University.

From 1973-78 he operated The Gallery, 65a Lisson Street, staging   projects with John Latham, Vaughan Grylls, Rita Donagh and others. Since then he worked as a teacher, writer, publisher and artist.

With Anna Douglas he co-authored *Artists Stories* (A-n 1996). Other published titles include *Interviews-Artists, Curators and Collections, Small Histories, The Ring of Minos* and *Albion Journal*. With Sarah Batiste he published *Cv Journal of Art & Crafts* 1988-91, forming *Cv Publications* in 1992 and *Cv/Visual Arts Research* in 1995. He is a member of the Royal Society of Oil Painters (ROI)

Studio Site:
www.tracksdirectory.ision.co.uk/candidarts

**ART . TRAVEL . HISTORIES .
SOCIAL STUDIES . STUDIO WORK**

Published by Cv Publications

www.tracksdirectory.ision.co.uk